creatures
of the sea

The
Whale
Shark

Other titles in the series:

creatures of the sea

The Whale Shark

Kris Hirschmann

KIDHAVEN
PRESS™

THOMSON

GALE

San Diego • Detroit • New York • San Francisco • Cleveland
New Haven, Conn. • Waterville, Maine • London • Munich

For more information, contact
KidHaven Press
27500 Drake Rd.
Farmington Hills, MI 48331-3535
Or you can visit our Internet site at http://www.gale.com

LIBRARY OF CONGRESS CATALOGING-IN-PUBLICATION DATA

Hirschmann, Kris, 1967–
  The Whale Shark / By Kristine Hirschmann.
  p. cm.—(Creatures of the sea)
Summary: Describes the physical characteristics, behavior, predators, and life cycle of the whale shark.
Includes bibliographical references and index.
  ISBN 0-7377-2059-X (Hardback : alk. paper)
1. Whale shark—Juvenile literature. [1. Whale shark. 2. Sharks.]

Table of Contents

Introduction

Mysterious Giants

There are close to four hundred types of sharks in the world. Of these, the largest by far is the whale shark. These enormous animals have captured the imagination of the public. They appear in many television documentaries—often with human divers tagging along. Their pictures are published in all sorts of magazines and books. Because of this publicity, whale sharks are among the world's most recognized shark species.

So it is surprising to realize how little is known about these creatures. Before the mid-1980s, only about three hundred whale shark sightings had ever been reported. Since that time, however, scientists have discovered that groups of whale sharks gather in certain places at certain times of the year. This discovery has allowed scientists to study these magnificent creatures for the first time. In the past two decades, more has been learned about the biology and habits of the whale shark.

Still, there is much that scientists do not know about whale sharks. For example, they have no idea how many whale sharks may exist in the world, or if whale sharks have home territories. Scientists do know that whale sharks sometimes travel long distances, but they are not sure whether these journeys are planned migrations or random wanderings. The reasons why whale sharks come together or

The whale shark is the largest shark in the world.

why they swim apart are still unknown, and there are many things about the whale shark's life cycle that scientists do not understand.

Scientists are working to find the answers to some of their questions. Researchers in Australia, Belize, the United States, and other places are doing this by attaching electronic tags to whale sharks. The tags send information about a whale shark's location, depth, speed, and more to satellites. The satellites then send the information to researchers' computers, where it can be studied and analyzed. Other ways of tracking whale sharks include acoustic tags, which send out sound signals, and plastic numbered tags that identify individual whale sharks.

Unfortunately tagging does not work very well. Tags of all types tend to come loose, so scientists usually gather only a few days' worth of information each time they tag a shark. Still, tags have helped scientists to understand a little bit about whale sharks' movements and habits. With continued effort, scientists are sure to learn more and more about whale sharks, the ocean's mysterious giants.

The World's Biggest Fish

Whale sharks belong to the scientific class *Elasmobranchii,* which includes all sharks, rays, and skates. The scientific name of the whale shark is **Rhincodon typus.** *Rhincodon* comes from a Greek word meaning "snout" or "nose." The whale shark got this name because of its wide, flat snout. No other shark's head looks quite like that of the whale shark.

The nickname "whale shark" comes from this animal's size. Typical whale sharks measure twenty-five to thirty feet from nose to tail. And the biggest whale sharks may be sixty feet from tip to tip—longer than most types of whales. No sixty-foot whale shark has ever been weighed, but scientists believe a creature of this size would tip the scales at twenty tons or perhaps even more.

Like all sharks, whale sharks are fish. Indeed, they are the world's biggest fish. No other fish species comes close to matching the whale shark's monstrous size.

Finding Whale Sharks

Whale sharks prefer water temperatures between seventy and eighty degrees Fahrenheit. For this reason they stick to tropical and temperate (cool but not cold) seas. Whale sharks seldom travel farther than a latitude of thirty degrees north or thirty-five degrees south of the equator.

Within this comfort zone, whale sharks can be found nearly everywhere around the globe. They roam through many parts of the Atlantic, Pacific, and Indian oceans. They may also wander into the Red Sea, which separates Africa from the Arabian Peninsula; the Gulf of Mexico, which lies between the United States and Central America; and other enclosed areas. In fact the only warm sea in which whale sharks are not found is the Mediterranean. This is probably because whale sharks would have to swim through an uncomfortably cold stretch of the Atlantic Ocean to reach this sea.

Whale sharks spend most of their lives far from land. They cruise the deep waters of the world by themselves. Occasionally whale sharks gather in

A family points to a whale shark in an aquarium in Japan. Whale sharks are the world's biggest fish.

groups of up to one hundred individuals, but schools of this size are very rare. Whale sharks are usually seen traveling alone.

Sometimes whale sharks come into shallower waters. These animals are most commonly seen along the coasts of Australia, Japan, Taiwan, India, the Philippines, Belize, Honduras, and Mexico. They are also spotted in the Caribbean, the Maldives, the Galápagos Islands, and a handful of other areas around the world.

The Whale Shark Shape

Apart from their size, whale sharks have many features that make them easy to recognize. One such feature is the front of the whale shark's head, which flattens into a broad snout. A wide mouth cuts straight across the front of the snout. This feature is very unusual among sharks, whose mouths are usually found on the underside of the head. Two small eyes are also found on the whale shark's head, one near each end of the mouth.

From the snout, the head slopes up sharply and joins a long, thick body. The body tapers evenly toward the tail. The whale shark's tail has one very large lobe on top and a much smaller lobe below. When the tail is waved back and forth through the water, it creates a strong push that shoves the whale shark forward. It is like a giant paddle that generates all of the shark's swimming power.

Whale sharks are easy to recognize by their flat, broad snouts.

On the whale shark's back are two **dorsal fins**. The first dorsal fin is large and roughly triangular in shape. The second dorsal fin (found near the tail) is much smaller. Both fins act as rudders to keep the whale shark stable in the water as it swims.

The whale shark's underside also has fins. Just behind and to the bottom of the head are two **pectoral fins**, one on each side of the shark's body. The whale shark can move these fins up and down and twist them slightly. Changing the position of the pectoral fins helps the shark to steer and to slow down when necessary. The shark's underside also has small stabilizing fins that are found directly beneath the first and second dorsal fins.

Distinctive Skin

The whale shark's skin is another feature that makes this animal easy to recognize. On the shark's upper surface, fins, and tail, the skin is dark gray or dark blue with vivid spots and bars. The spots and bars are usually white or yellow and are arranged in a checkerboard pattern. Each whale shark has slightly different markings and can be identified by its unique skin pattern.

Whale sharks have distinctive patterns of spots and bars on their upper bodies.

The bottom of the whale shark's body is white. This body pattern (darker on top, lighter on the bottom) is called **countershading**. Countershading makes a swimming animal hard to see from any direction. From above, the animal seems to fade into the dark ocean depths. From below, it disappears against the sunny sea surface.

Scientists are not sure why the whale shark has such striking colors. Most animals use color patterns to keep themselves from being seen by predators. But because the whale shark is so big, it has no natural enemies. There does not seem to be any reason for this huge animal to hide. Perhaps whale sharks were smaller many millions of years ago. If so, their skin color might be left over from a more dangerous time. Scientists also point out that whale sharks spend a lot of time near the ocean's surface. They wonder if this animal's colors might somehow protect it from the sun's rays.

A Tough Covering

Color is not the only important feature of the whale shark's skin. The skin also serves as a tough covering that protects the shark's inner organs. In some places a whale shark's skin may be four inches thick. Very few animals or objects can rip a hole through this armor.

The whale shark's thick skin is coated with thousands upon thousands of tiny, backward-pointing teeth called **dermal denticles**. The denticles are arranged in overlapping layers, much like the scales of a fish. Unlike scales, however, the denticles are molded into bony bumps and ridges. These bumps and ridges are too small to see from even a few feet away. But they can easily be felt. Touching a whale shark's skin is like rubbing rough sandpaper. If rubbed too hard against the grain, the dermal denticles can scratch or tear human flesh.

Dermal denticles may help the whale shark swim more easily. As a whale shark moves through the ocean, the denticles' ridges break the water into little streams that flow around the shark's body. This has the effect of **streamlining** the shark. Three raised ridges along each side of a whale shark's body also help to streamline this enormous animal.

On the Move

Streamlining is important to an animal that is always on the move. Whale sharks swim constantly from the moment they are born until the day they die. They do not move quickly; the typical whale shark speed is be-

tween three and five miles per hour. These huge creatures move slowly forward, their bodies swaying back and forth as they wave their powerful tails.

Even at slow speeds, the whale shark can cover huge distances. Scientists know that most whale sharks cover thousands of miles during their lifetimes. Traveling from one part of the world to another

Whale sharks swim constantly and typically travel between three and five miles per hour.

Prefering sunlight and warmth, whale sharks usually travel near the ocean's surface.

might take several years for these slow-moving creatures.

Wherever they travel, whale sharks usually stay near the ocean's surface. Although these animals can dive as deep as three thousand feet if necessary, they are sure to pop back up to shallower regions before long. Whale sharks seem to feel most at home in a world of sunlight and warmth. If the ocean is calm, they may even swim so close to the surface that their dorsal fins jut into the air. These giant fins cut the water, creating a wake that marks the shark's passage. This wake, along with the fins that caused it, is a visible reminder that the world's biggest fish is passing just below.

2

Life Cycle

No one knows exactly how long whale sharks live. Some scientists think whale sharks live no longer than 60 years. Others believe these animals may live as long as 150 years. All estimates, however, are just guesses. So far, a whale shark has never been tracked all the way from birth to death.

The only way of estimating a whale shark's age is by its size. Smaller sharks are younger, and larger sharks are older. A sixty-foot whale shark is a very old shark indeed. It has lived a full life that includes birth, growth, and adulthood, and it has probably produced thousands of babies of its own.

Unanswered Questions

Age is not the only unanswered question about the whale shark's life cycle. Scientists are still trying to find out many other things about these little-known animals. For example, because no one has ever seen whale sharks breed, no one knows exactly how male and female whale sharks find each other when it is time to mate. It is also unknown whether whale sharks do special things to attract each other, as many animals do. Scientists have been able to see loose schools of up to one hundred whale sharks. Perhaps breeding happens during these rare times when whale sharks come together in groups.

Scientists also do not know whether whale sharks have regular seasons or areas for breeding. However, newborn whale sharks have been caught

No one knows how long whale sharks live. Scientists can only estimate a whale shark's age by its size.

off the western coast of Central America, in the Marshall Islands, in the Gulf of Guinea, in the Persian Gulf, off the coast of Taiwan, and in other regions. Some of these areas are far apart. This suggests that breeding takes place all over the world. Newborn whale sharks have been caught during many different times of the year, so breeding probably takes place all year round.

Another mystery is how whale shark "society" works. There could be just one worldwide population of whale sharks, any of which may breed with any other. Or there could be separate groups of whale sharks in different parts of the world that do not mix with other groups. Some scientists have suggested testing the genetic material of whale sharks from different parts of the world to see if they are related. If so, it would give scientists an important clue about the lifestyle of the whale shark.

Mating

Although no one has ever seen whale sharks mating, scientists believe that the process is the same one used by other sharks. Like all sharks, male whale sharks have two organs called **claspers** on the undersides of their bodies. These organs are used to insert sperm into an opening in the female's underside. Once inside the female, the sperm may fertilize eggs. This starts the growth process. The combined eggs and sperm will develop into baby sharks.

Whale sharks are difficult to study in the wild, so scientists know very little about the shark's life cycle.

Different sharks behave differently during the mating process. In many shark species, males use their teeth to bite and hold onto their mates while they breed. But whale sharks do not have biting teeth. There is no way for a male to hold onto the female. Therefore mating is probably done belly to belly. It is probably over very quickly.

In most shark species, males and females go their separate ways as soon as they are done mating. The male does not stay with the female or help her in any way during her pregnancy. Whale sharks are not known to travel in male-female pairs, so they probably follow the typical shark pattern of separation after mating.

Because whale sharks do not travel in male-female pairs, scientists believe the sharks separate after mating.

Developing Babies

Some sharks lay eggs. Egg-laying sharks are called **oviparous**. Other sharks carry egg cases inside their bodies until they hatch, then give birth to live babies. Sharks that produce young in this manner are called **ovoviviparous**.

Until recently scientists believed that whale sharks were oviparous. They believed this because in 1953, a large egg case containing an unborn whale shark was found in the Gulf of Mexico. In 1995, however, a female shark carrying about three hundred embryos (developing babies) was caught near Taiwan. This discovery proved that whale sharks are ovoviviparous. Scientists now think that the egg case found in 1953 probably accidentally came out of the mother's body too early.

Female whale sharks have two uteruses, or wombs. Many embryos develop at the same time within each uterus. In the beginning each embryo is surrounded and protected by a thick, foot-long case. Inside the case is a large yolk to which the embryo is attached. The embryo uses this yolk for energy, slowly absorbing the yolk as it grows. Over time the yolk gets smaller and smaller and the developing shark gets larger and larger. Before long the embryo is about two feet long. Its body is bent and twisted inside the protective case. The only

Female whale sharks carry hundreds of embryos at a time and give birth to live babies.

sign of the yolk is a small cord attached to the embryo's underside.

At this point the embryo is ready to hatch from its case. Still within the mother shark's uterus, the embryo breaks loose. Soon it leaves the mother's body, along with its brothers and sisters. For several months after it is born, the young shark (which is called a **pup**) bears a round scar on its underside that shows where the yolk was attached.

On Their Own

Most sharks do not take care of their pups after birth. It is therefore likely that young whale sharks leave their mothers as soon as they are born. No one has to teach the pups how to swim or eat. They already have all the tools and knowledge they need to make their way in the world alone.

Just because a whale shark pup knows how to swim and eat, however, does not mean it is safe. Young whale sharks are much smaller than adults, so they are often attacked by larger animals. Great whites, tiger sharks, blue sharks, and other big species might eat baby whale sharks. Large predatory fish such as blue marlins have also been found with whale shark pups in their stomachs. Between sharks, marlins, and other predators, a huge number of whale sharks are eaten early in life. Scientists believe that as few as 10 percent of all whale sharks survive to adulthood.

The most dangerous time for a whale shark pup is right after birth. At this time the shark is at its

When whale sharks are young, they are vulnerable to predators and few survive to reach adulthood.

smallest and weakest. Very soon, however, the young whale shark begins to grow. Whale shark eggs have hatched in aquariums, so scientists know that babies go through an enormous growth spurt—perhaps tripling in length—during their first five months of life.

After the first early growth spurt, the young whale shark's rate of growth slows dramatically. From now on the shark will grow steadily. It will continue to grow throughout its life, getting longer and heavier until the day it finally dies.

Becoming Adults

It takes whale sharks a long time to reach adulthood. Scientists believe that these animals are not able to mate and create babies of their own until they reach a length of twenty-five to thirty feet. It may be twenty years or more before a whale shark finally gets this big.

Once they reach maturity, female whale sharks probably give birth to a new batch of pups every two to three years. Adult males probably mate whenever they get the opportunity. In this way, both males and females do their part to create a new generation of whale sharks to populate the world's oceans.

3

Whale Sharks as Predator and Prey

Whale sharks can be a frightening sight. A big whale shark dwarfs even the largest human, and it is powerful enough to bat a swimmer aside with one sweep of its mighty tail. Its enormous mouth opens so wide that it seems a person could disappear inside, never to be seen again.

But despite its alarming appearance, the whale shark is actually one of the ocean's gentlest creatures. These animals are not hunters. They are **filter feeders**, which means they eat by sucking in ocean water and gobbling down any small animals that happen to wash into their mouths. Whale sharks eat mostly **plankton**, which is a mixture of

In spite of their frightening appearance, whale sharks are gentle creatures.

algae, bacteria, and tiny developing animals. They will also eat jellyfish, squids, and little fish.

Finding Food

Whale sharks must eat a great deal of food every day to get the energy they need to power their huge bodies. For this reason, whale sharks stick to waters that contain plenty of plankton. Although no one knows for sure, most scientists do not believe whale sharks have a home territory. Rather, they swim wherever the search for food takes them. This search may cause a whale shark to travel thousands of miles in a single year.

Some areas are rich in food all year long. Currents that flow near continents, for example, are full of the nutrients that plankton need to thrive. Such currents exist off the California coast and along the west coasts of southern Africa and South America. All of these areas are visited often by whale sharks.

Other areas have seasonal food "bursts" that attract whale sharks at certain times of the year. One such area is Australia's 160-mile-long Ningaloo Reef.

Whale sharks eat mostly plankton and any small animals that wash into their mouths.

Each year in late March or early April, the coral polyps that live on this reef spawn. They release uncountable millions of egg packets along with sperm intended to fertilize the packets. The spawn fills the water with pure protein—the perfect food for a hungry whale shark. Hundreds of whale sharks show up each year to take advantage of this feast.

Gladden Spit in Belize is another whale shark gathering spot. In April and May, thousands of snappers arrive at Gladden Spit to spawn. Their activity releases a cloud of eggs and sperm into the water. Large numbers of whale sharks arrive soon afterward to slurp down the tasty soup.

Using the Senses

Whale sharks find plankton by using their sharp senses. Smell is the most important sense. Whale sharks smell by taking water into an opening just above the snout. Inside this opening, nerve endings pick up odors floating in the water. The nerve endings send messages to the brain, which "reads" the messages to see what kind of food is on the menu.

A whale shark can also use its sense of smell to find the thickest part of a plankton cloud. It swings its head back and forth in the water, "sniffing" to see where the scent is strongest. The shark changes direction constantly to keep swimming toward plankton-rich areas. Before long the hungry whale shark is surrounded by food.

Whale sharks use their keen sense of smell to find plankton-rich waters.

Like all sharks, whale sharks also have an additional "super sense" that helps them find food. This sense allows whale sharks to feel the electrical fields created by living creatures. They detect these fields with pits called **ampullae of Lorenzini** that line the undersides of their snouts. Whale sharks can use this "electro-sense," along with their sense of smell, to find food at night. They may also use it to help them find their way back to certain feeding grounds year after year. How? It is possible that these animals can read the earth's magnetic fields, much like humans might read an enormous map.

Scientists do not think vision is important to the whale shark. Whale sharks can see, but their eyes are very small compared to their bodies. The eyes are also located on the sides of the shark's head, making it difficult to see directly ahead. It would be very hard for a whale shark to find food if it had to rely on its eyesight alone.

Eating a Meal

Unlike most sharks, whale sharks do not have large teeth. Instead they have many tiny teeth measuring no more than one-quarter inch each. These little teeth are arranged in long rows. A large whale shark may have three hundred rows of teeth in both its top and bottom jaws, for a total of up to six thousand teeth. All of these teeth are covered by flaps of skin, making them harmless. The whale shark's teeth do not seem to have any role in the eating process.

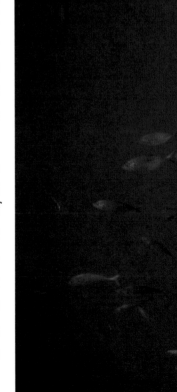

Instead of using their teeth, whale sharks eat by filtering small plants and animals out of the water. A whale shark first brings seawater into its enormous mouth, which may be six feet wide and two feet tall when it is fully open. The shark then shuts its mouth tight. It forces the water out through large openings called **gill slits** that are found just behind the head, five on each side of the body. The insides of the gill slits are covered by structures called **gill rakers**, which are a combination of crisscrossed cartilage and spongy material. Water passes easily through the gill rakers, but anything larger than about an eighth of an inch across does not. Plankton and other food items are trapped against the inside of the gill rakers like pasta in a sieve.

When open, a whale shark's mouth can be as much as six feet wide and two feet high.

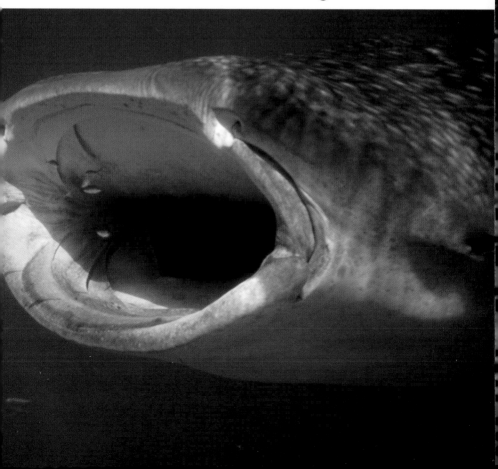

When all water has been forced out of the mouth, the whale shark swallows any food it has trapped. After swallowing, the whale shark opens its mouth again and takes in another huge gulp of seawater. Then it closes its mouth, forces the water out through the gills, and swallows once more. A whale shark may repeat this action twenty times per minute when it is actively eating.

Every once in a while a whale shark takes in a larger animal, such as a tuna or another big fish. The whale shark usually tries to eat whatever it catches. It may succeed in getting the fish down its throat and digesting it—or it may not. If a whale shark swallows something it cannot digest, it just pokes its stomach inside out through its mouth to eject the unwanted food. Then it pulls its stomach back in and returns to its normal routine.

Active and Passive Feeding

Whale sharks have two ways of feeding. The first way is passive. A whale shark that is feeding passively simply swims along with its mouth partly open, letting food-rich water wash inside. Every now and then the shark closes its mouth, forces water out through the gills, and swallows anything that remains in its mouth. It does not go out of its way to find food. It just takes whatever comes its way.

Active feeding is a more common method. A whale shark that is feeding actively does not simply

Whale sharks feed by gulping huge amounts of seawater and filtering out plankton and small animals.

let water wash into its mouth. Instead it uses suction power to pull water in. By doing this the shark captures any small creatures that might be trying to swim away. It also takes in a bigger cloud of food in a single gulp.

Active feeding is often seen when whale sharks find an especially thick fog of plankton. A whale shark may swim back and forth through a food-rich area, waving its head from side to side and sucking repeatedly to get as much food as possible. The cloudy water clears as the shark passes and the food disappears down its giant throat.

Sometimes a whale shark even stops in one place to gather as much food as possible. It hangs tail-down in the water with its huge mouth near the surface. Then it bobs up and down as it swallows a mass of plankton one mouthful at a time. Like an enormous vacuum cleaner, the whale shark sucks up everything in its path. It will leave when its belly is full or when the plankton is gone, whichever comes first.

Whale Sharks as Prey

No sea creature will attack a full-grown whale shark. However, humans can and sometimes do kill these gigantic animals. In recent years, whale shark flesh has become a popular food in some parts of the world. As a result whale sharks today are being killed in record numbers. Fishermen in one small area in India, for example, took as many as one thousand whale sharks from the sea between 1999 and 2000. And fishermen kill an estimated one hundred whale sharks near Taiwan each year.

Most whale sharks caught by fishermen are less than twenty-five feet long. Whale sharks of this length are not yet mature. The fact that so few mature whale sharks are being caught means trouble. It suggests that not very many adults are left. And if only a few adults are left to create new babies, then whale shark populations may drop.

Whale shark flesh is popular food in some parts of the world, and fishermen kill hundreds of the creatures every year.

In late 2002, the United Nations Convention on International Trade in Endangered Species (CITES) placed the whale shark under international observation. This ruling means that countries participating in the CITES program must prove that their actions do not harm whale shark populations. This is an important step forward in the protection of whale sharks, which currently are considered "vulnerable" (not yet endangered but at risk of extinction in the future if conditions do not change). What will become of this gentle giant of the sea? Only time and further research will tell.

Glossary

ampullae of Lorenzini: Organs that sense electrical fields, including the weak signals given off by all living creatures.

claspers: The external sexual organs of the male whale shark.

countershading: Coloration that is darker on top and lighter on the bottom.

dermal denticles: Tiny toothlike scales that cover a whale shark's skin.

dorsal fins: Fins that stick up from the back.

Elasmobranchii: The scientific class that includes all sharks, rays, and skates.

filter feeder: An animal that feeds by filtering small edible particles from the water.

gill rakers: Sievelike organs that trap food inside the whale shark's mouth.

gill slits: Vertical slits on both sides of the whale shark's body. Water leaves the whale shark's mouth through the gill slits.

oviparous: A shark that lays eggs.

ovoviviparous: A shark that carries eggs inside its body until they hatch, then gives birth to live young.

pectoral fins: Fins that stick out on each side of the shark.

plankton: A soup of algae, bacteria, and developing creatures that floats in many shallow parts of the ocean. The main food of whale sharks.

pup: A baby shark.

Rhincodon typus: The scientific name of the whale shark.

streamlined: Shaped in a way that reduces resistance when moving through water.

Books

Amanda Harman, *Endangered! Sharks.* Tarrytown, NY: Benchmark Books, 1996. This book introduces readers to three threatened shark species: great whites, whale sharks, and basking sharks.

Christopher Maynard, *Informania: Sharks.* Cambridge, MA: Candlewick Press, 1997. A fun layout makes this book exciting to read, as well as informative. Read about many species of sharks.

Periodical

Eugenie Clark, "Whale Sharks: Gentle Monsters of the Deep," *National Geographic*, December 1992. This article focuses on the whale sharks of Australia's Ningaloo Reef.

Website

Island of the Sharks (www.pbs.org/wgbh/nova/sharks). Includes information on many different types of sharks, including whale sharks. The site also has an "Ask the Experts" section where readers can submit questions.

Video

Erin N. Calmes, *The Whale Shark Hunters*. Pro-Active Entertainment, 2003. This *National Geographic* documentary follows actor William Shatner on a journey to swim with whale sharks in Mexico.

index

picture credits

Cover image: © James Watt/AnimalsAnimals/
  Earth Scenes
A.N.T./Photo Researchers, Inc., 37
Hitoshi Maeshiro/EPA/Landov, 11
Fred McConnaughey/Photo Researchers, Inc., 25
© Amos Nachoum/CORBIS, 14, 31, 34–35
© Jeffrey L. Rotman/CORBIS, 13
© James Watt/Visuals Unlimited, 7, 16–17, 18,
  21, 24, 27, 30, 33, 38–39
© Lawson Wood/CORBIS, 23

about the author

Kris Hirschmann has written more than one hundred books for children. She is the president of The Wordshop, a business that provides a variety of writing and editorial services. She holds a bachelor's degree in psychology from Dartmouth College in Hanover, New Hampshire. Hirschmann lives just outside Orlando, Florida, with her husband, Michael, and her daughter, Nikki.

2/06